AMICUS ILLUSTRATED • AMICUS INK

DO YOU REALLY WANT TO MEET A HIPPOPOTAMUS?

WRITTEN BY BRIDGET HEOS   ILLUSTRATED BY DANIELE FABBRI

Amicus Illustrated and Amicus Ink
are imprints of Amicus
P.O. Box 1329
Mankato, MN 56002

Library of Congress Cataloging-in-Publication Data
Heos, Bridget, author.
 Do you really want to meet a hippopotamus? / by
Bridget Heos ; illustrated by Daniele Fabbri.
   pages cm. – (Do you really want to meet...wild
animals?)
 Audience: K to grade 3.
 Summary: "A boy travels to Africa, observes hippo-
potamuses in the wild, and learns how dangerous
they can be when defending their herds"– Provided
by publisher.
 ISBN 978-1-60753-946-9 (library binding) –
 ISBN 978-1-68152-117-6 (pbk.) –
 ISBN 978-1-68151-064-4 (ebook)
 1. Hippopotamus–Behavior–Juvenile literature.
 2. Hippopotamus–Juvenile literature. I. Fabbri,
Daniele, 1978- illustrator. II. Title.
 QL737.U57H46 2016
 599.63'5–dc23   2015029357

Editor: Rebecca Glaser
Designer : Kathleen Petelinsek

Printed in the United States of America at Corporate
Graphics in North Mankato, Minnesota.

HC 10 9 8 7 6 5 4 3 2 1
PB 10 9 8 7 6 5 4 3 2 1

ABOUT THE AUTHOR

Bridget Heos lives in Kansas City with her husband, four
children, and an extremely dangerous cat . . . to mice,
anyway. She has written more than 80 books for children,
including many about animals. Find out more about her at
www.authorbridgetheos.com.

ABOUT THE ILLUSTRATOR

Daniele Fabbri was born in Ravenna, Italy, in 1978. He
graduated from Istituto Europeo di Design in Milan, Italy,
and started his career as a cartoon animator, storyboarder,
and background designer for animated series. He has
worked as a freelance illustrator since 2003, collaborating
with international publishers and advertising agencies.

A hippopotamus is a huge creature. You want to see one in the wild? Wait. Did you know that hippos are more dangerous than lions, leopards, or crocodiles?

When people get too close to hippos, they charge. That's bad, because hippos weigh up to 8,000 pounds (3,629 kg). And they can run as fast as humans!

If a hippo charges you, your only hope is to climb a tree. Hippos don't climb. Do you *really* want to meet a hippo?

Okay, let's go. All wild hippos live in Africa. Better pack
a good book! The flight will take more than a full day!

Here we are in South Africa. The best place
to see hippos is on the river. Climb on board!

There they are! Hippos are social animals and
live in herds, so you'll see several at a time,
wallowing in shallow water to stay cool.

Hippos have nostrils on top of their noses. This lets them breathe while being mostly underwater. You're hot, too? Well, don't get in with the hippos!

Hippos will fight any animal—or person—who gets too close. And when hippos fight, they bite! Hippo teeth can grow to 20 inches (50 cm)! Ouch! Uh-oh, a hippo is heading your way. It looks like it's yawning, but it's not tired. When a hippo shows its big teeth, it's a threat.

Don't worry. It's not threatening you. It's going after that crocodile!
Usually hippos and crocodiles live in the same habitat.

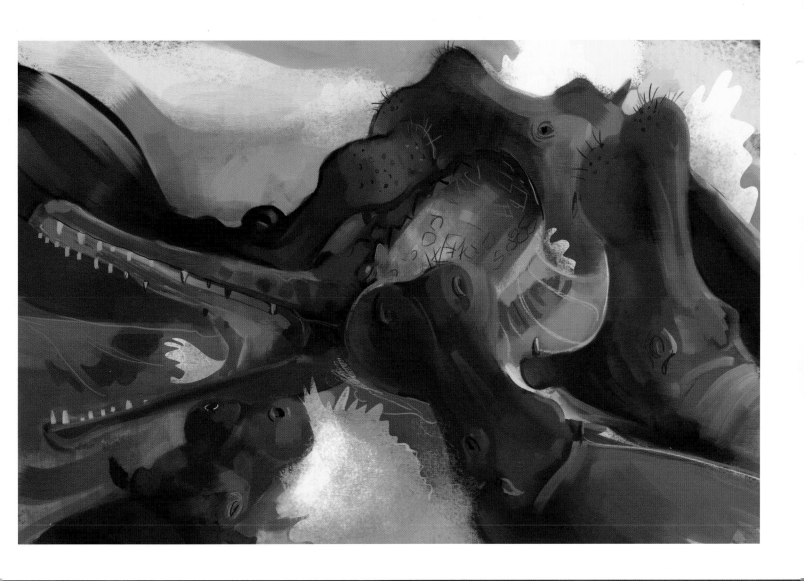

But crocodiles sometimes prey on baby hippos. So
if a crocodile gets too close . . . Chomp! Youch!

The crocodile gets away. It survived the attack because
of its thick skin. Why is the hippo yawning now?

It's threatening the other hippo. Male hippos fight over who can be the dominant hippo. The winner gets to boss the other males around.

But the female hippos are the
leaders of the whole herd.
They care for the young hippos.
Mama and baby hippos love
to play and snuggle! Aww . . .
the baby hippo is so cute!

But don't try to reach out and pet it! Hippo mamas are sweet to their babies. They're not so sweet when you get close to their babies.

It's getting late. When it cools off at night, the hippos leave the water to find food. Hippos are herbivores. They follow paths to find grass and other plants, and they eat for several hours.

Should you follow them?
No, better not! It's best to meet
hippos from a distance.

Good-bye, hippos!

WHERE DO HIPPOPOTAMUSES LIVE?

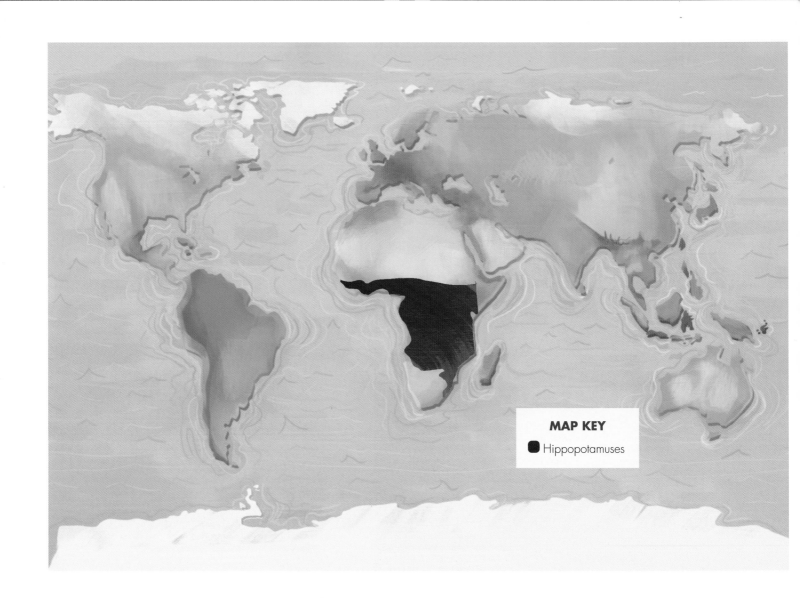

MAP KEY

● Hippopotamuses

GLOSSARY

dominant Being in charge, as when one is the boss of other hippos, and so gets the best mates, food, wallowing spots, and more.

herbivore An animal that eats mostly plants.

herd A group of the same kind of animals.

social Living in groups; social animals like hippos take care of each other.

wallow To lie in mud or water.

READ MORE

London, Jonathan. *Hippos Are Huge!* Somerville, Mass.: Candlewick Press, 2015.

Lunis, Natalie. **Hippopotamus**. New York: Bearport, 2016.

Owings, Lisa. **Meet a Baby Hippo**. Minneapolis: Lerner, 2015.

Riggs, Kate. *Hippopotamuses*. Mankato, Minn.: Creative Education, 2016.

WEBSITES

National Geographic Kids: Animals: Hippopotamus
http://kids.nationalgeographic.com/content/kids/en_US/animals/hippopotamus/
Learn more about hippos.

National Geographic: Animals: Nile Crocodile
http://animals.nationalgeographic.com/animals/reptiles/nile-crocodile/
Read about hippos' tough neighbors, Nile crocodiles.

St. Louis Zoo: About the Animals: Nile Hippopotamus
http://www.stlzoo.org/animals/abouttheanimals/mammals/hoofedmammals/hippopotamus/
Learn about hippos' appetites, fighting males, and more.

Every effort has been made to ensure that these websites are appropriate for children. However, because of the nature of the Internet, it is impossible to guarantee that these sites will remain active indefinitely or that their contents will not be altered.